TIMELINE HISTORY

# TRANSPORTATION

## From Walking to High-Speed Rail

Elizabeth Raum

Heinemann Library
Chicago, Illinois

## www.heinemannraintree.com

Visit our website to find out more information about Heinemann-Raintree books.

## To order:

☎ Phone 888-454-2279

💻 Visit www.heinemannraintree.com to browse our catalog and order online.

Edited by Louise Galpine and Diyan Leake
Designed by Richard Parker
Original illustrations © Capstone Global Library Ltd 2011
Illustrated by Jeff Edwards
Picture research by Hannah Taylor

Originated by Dot Gradations Ltd
Printed and bound in China by CTPS

14 13 12 11 10
10 9 8 7 6 5 4 3 2 1

**Library of Congress Cataloging-in-Publication Data**
Raum, Elizabeth.
  Transportation : from walking to high speed rail / Elizabeth Raum.
    p. cm. -- (Timeline history)
  Includes bibliographical references and index.
  ISBN 978-1-4329-3804-8 (hc) -- ISBN 978-1-4329-3812-3 (pb)  1. Transportation engineering--Juvenile literature. 2. Transportation--Juvenile literature.  I. Title.
  TA1149.R38 2011
  629.04--dc22
                            2009048960

**Acknowledgments**
The author and publisher are grateful to the following for permission to reproduce copyright material:  Alamy Images pp. **5** top (© SCPhotos), **12** (© Interfoto), **24** (© RIA Novosti); Corbis pp. **4** (Harrison Schmitt), **6** (Bettmann), **8** (Bettmann), **11** top (Fine Art Photographic Library), **14** bottom (Bettmann), **15** (Bettmann), **19** top (Bettmann), **20** (Bettmann), **22** bottom (Bettmann); Getty Images pp. **7** bottom (The Bridgeman Art Library), **10** (The Bridgeman Art Library/Look & Learn), **11** bottom (SSPL), **18** (SSPL), **19** bottom (Hulton Archive), **21** bottom (New York Times Co.), **22** top (Hulton Archive), **23** (Fox Photos/M. McNeill), **25** bottom (AFP/Simon Maina), **26** (Bloomberg/Peter Frommenwiler); Library of Congress pp. **14** top, **16** top; Mary Evans pp. **13** top (©Rue des Archives), **9** bottom, **16** bottom; NASA pp. **25** top, **27** bottom (Steve Lee University of Colorado, Jim Bell Cornell University); Photolibrary pp. **7** top (North Wind Pictures), **9** top (Steve Vidler), **13** bottom (The Print Collector), **17** (The Print Collector), **21** top, **27** top (Othk Othk).

Cover photograph of a high-speed train reproduced with permission of Shutterstock (© Aleksi Markku).

Every effort has been made to contact copyright holders of material reproduced in this book. Any omissions will be rectified in subsequent printings if notice is given to the publisher.

# Contents

Historical time is divided into two major periods. BCE is short for "Before the Common Era"—that is, the time before the Christian religion began. This is the time up to the year 1 BCE. CE is short for "Common Era." This means the time from the year 1 BCE to the present. For example, when a date is given as 1000 CE, it is 1,000 years after the year 1 BCE. The abbreviation *c.* stands for *circa*, which is Latin for "around."

Any words appearing in the text in bold, **like this**, are explained in the glossary.

# What Is Transportation?

Transportation is the way people and goods move from place to place. We travel on foot, by bicycle, or in a car. In cities, public transportation includes buses, trams, and trains. Ships, planes, and spacecraft make it possible for people and goods to travel great distances.

The **moon rover** carried astronauts across the surface of the moon in the 1970s.

## Trade

Transportation allows us to trade with other people, and trade allows for the growth of towns and cities. Transportation brings farm goods and building materials to the cities, where they are traded for other goods. In early times, travel and trade were slow and difficult. Today, it is possible to travel all over the world by land, sea, or air.

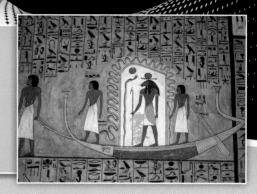

For thousands of years, people have used boats to travel from place to place, as shown in this painting from ancient Egypt.

# Timelines

The information in this book is on a timeline. A timeline shows you events from history in the order they happened. The big timeline in the middle of each page gives you details of a certain time in history (see below).

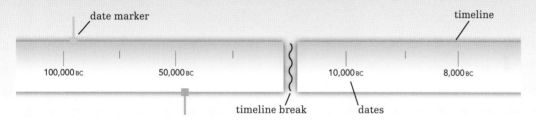

date marker

timeline

100,000 BC          50,000 BC          10,000 BC          8,000 BC

timeline break          dates

Some dates are exact. For example, in the year 1969 people first walked on the moon. Others are more general because early people did not keep written records. The smaller timeline at the bottom of each page shows you how the page you are reading fits into history as a whole. You will read about transportation all around the world. Each entry on the main timeline is in a different color. This color shows you which continent the information is about. The map below shows you how this color coding works. Pale green indicates events that took place on more than one continent or worldwide.

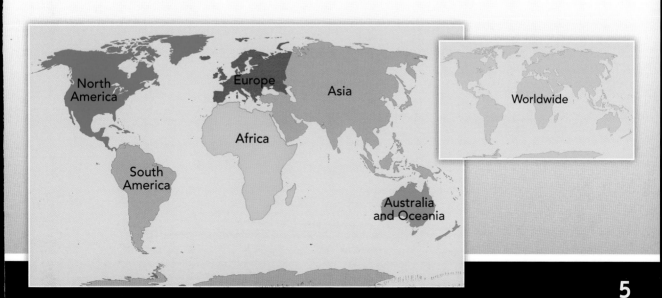

North America

Europe

Asia

Worldwide

Africa

South America

Australia and Oceania

# Beginning to Travel

Early people walked great distances gathering food and hunting. Gradually, people moved from Africa to Asia and Europe. The invention of boats and wheels allowed people to travel even farther and to carry heavier loads.

**c. 98,000 BCE**
Early people dragged things from place to place.

| 100,000 BCE | 50,000 BCE | 10,000 BCE | 8,000 BCE |

**c. 53,000 BCE**
Early people used rafts made of sticks to travel hundreds of miles from Southeast Asia to Australia.

**c. 6,000 BCE**
Dugout canoes carried people along China's longest river, the Yangtze. A dugout is a boat made from a hollowed-out tree trunk.

**c. 5,000 BCE**
In North Africa, people used camels and donkeys to carry loads.

**c. 4,000 BCE**

The Phoenicians, a **civilization** in the **Middle East**, sailed the Mediterranean Sea in long wooden rowboats with room for 15 to 20 rowers on each side.

**c. 3,300 BCE**

Egyptians tied bundles of **reeds** together to make boats. A reed roof kept sailors dry.

6,000 BCE          4,000 BCE          2,000 BCE

**c. 3,500 BCE    ROLLING ALONG**

No one knows exactly when the wheel was invented. It probably began as a rolling log. People made the first wheels by tying three flat boards side by side and carving them into a circle. Later, they used stone or clay. By the 1300s BCE, they were used on **chariots** in Egypt (right).

# Picking Up Speed

By about 2000 BCE, people in Egypt, China, and Scandinavia made lighter, larger wheels with **spokes.** Wheels with spokes were easier to pull long distances.

*c.* 2000–1500 BCE
**Chariots** were light, fast, two-wheeled carts pulled by horses. They helped the Egyptians win wars.

*c.* 400 BCE
The trireme, a high-speed wooden warship used by the Greeks and Romans, had space for 170 men to sit and row.

*c.* 100 CE
The Chinese invented the **wheelbarrow,** a single-wheeled **vehicle** with handles used to carry heavy loads.

2000 BCE

400 BCE    200 BCE    1 BCE    200 CE

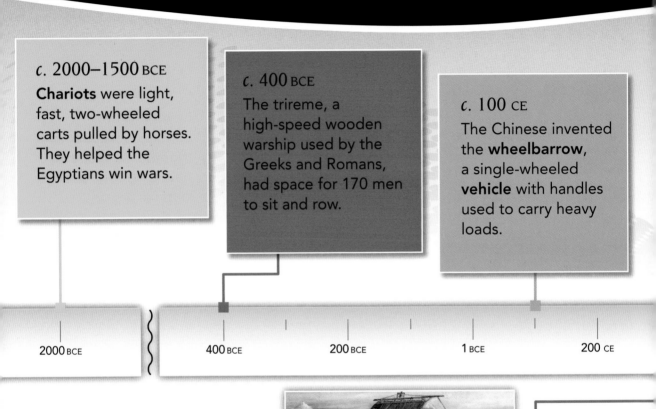

*c.* 700 CE   SPEEDY SHIPS
The Vikings lived in what is now called Denmark, Norway, and Sweden. They built speedy ships made from the wood of oak trees. Both ends of the boat often were the same so that the ship did not have to turn around in narrow rivers or small harbors. Vikings used their warships to raid cities and towns throughout Europe.

## *c.* 800 CE

During the T'ang **dynasty**, Chinese traders increased the use of boats called junks to carry goods to markets abroad. Junks had a hull (lower part) that was divided into sections for **cargo**.

## *c.* 900–1000 CE

Horses could travel farther and pull heavier loads once iron horseshoes and harnesses were improved.

| 400 CE | 600 CE | 800 CE | 1000 CE |

# Facing Dangers at Sea

Traveling across the world's oceans was especially dangerous for slaves and prisoners forced onto ships. At least two million Africans died on slave ships because of illness or lack of food and water.

## 1492

Christopher Columbus sailed from Spain to America in the *Santa Maria*, a **carrack**. His other ships, the *Niña* and the *Pinta*, were **caravels**. These ships were sturdy enough for long ocean voyages.

1480    1530    1580    1630    1680

## 1500s–1800s

Slave ships made over 39,000 trips from Africa to America. The trip took two to four months. Many millions of Africans were taken to a life of captivity.

## Late 1600s–1850s  OVERLAND CANALS

Until the mid-1800s, people in Europe and North America hauled supplies on barges, which are large, flat-bottomed boats. Horses trudged along the banks of **canals** pulling the barges, which went through locks (right) when water levels changed. Workers dug the canals by hand. Early canals in England carried coal from mines to factories. By 1850 there were 7,200 kilometers (4,500 miles) of canals in the United States.

**1670**

In Great Britain, **stagecoaches** carried people between London and Edinburgh. The journey took two weeks. Stage coaches continued to be used in Britain into the 1900s.

**1787–1868**

Due to overcrowding in prisons, the British shipped 162,000 prisoners to Australia. The prisoners slept in chains and had barely enough room to stand up.

1730      1780      1830      1880

# Building Up Steam

James Watt of Scotland invented a working steam **engine** in 1765. For **energy**, steam engines used pressure (force) created by boiling water. Other inventors used Watt's steam engine to provide power for ships, trains, and cars.

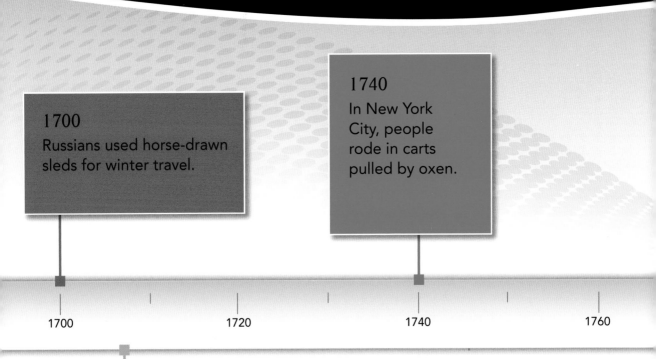

**1700**
Russians used horse-drawn sleds for winter travel.

**1740**
In New York City, people rode in carts pulled by oxen.

1700      1720      1740      1760

**1700s**
Miners traveled by canoe from São Paulo to gold mines in Minas Gerais, a state that has some of the biggest rivers in Brazil. Groups of 50 to 300 canoes made the trip in five to seven months.

**1769**
Nicolas-Joseph Cugnot of France invented a steam-powered **vehicle**. It traveled 3.6 kilometers (2¼ miles) per hour and stopped every 10 to 12 minutes to build up enough steam to keep going.

## 1800s

Steamboats carried passengers along rivers in Europe and the United States. Sometimes passengers were killed when steamboat engines blew up.

| 1780 | 1800 | 1820 |

## 1783 UP, UP, UP AND AWAY

A hot-air balloon landed in a small French village. The villagers thought it was a monster and attacked it with stones and pitchforks. Soon hot-air balloons became a regular sight. People used balloons for sightseeing, to predict the weather, and to observe enemies during wartime.

# Cruising the Oceans

During the mid-1800s, shipping companies offered passenger service across the oceans. Cruise ships provided nice rooms and tasty food for rich passengers. **Immigrant** ships, on the other hand, carried poor people from Europe to the United States. The ships were crowded, and often there was not enough food and water.

**1820s–1880s**
Over 9.5 million immigrants reached a new life in the United States by ship.

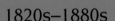

1820          1825          1830          1835

**1825**
The British engineer George Stephenson built a **locomotive** called the *Rocket*. It made future railroads possible.

## 1838

The *Great Western*, a ship designed by Isambard Kingdom Brunel, took passengers from Bristol, England, to New York City in 15 days.

## 1840s

Ships carried miners across the Atlantic and Pacific oceans to goldfields in California and Australia.

## 1850s–present

People in Bolivia used **reed** boats to travel around Lake Titicaca. They still use them today.

1840

1845

1850

## 1839   BICYCLES FOR EVERYONE

A Scottish **blacksmith** named Kirkpatrick Macmillan invented the first bicycle with pedals. In 1868 rubber tires and brakes were added. At first, adults had trouble learning to ride bicycles. Today, bicycles are used throughout the world. They are cheaper than cars and do not cause pollution.

# Chugging Along

During the 1800s, passenger service grew. Trains, subways, and rickshaws (two-wheeled carts that a person pulls) gave large numbers of people new ways to travel across a country or within cities.

## 1840–1880
In the United States, pioneers traveled by covered wagon to settle in the western part of the country.

1840            1845            1850            1855

## 1840–1907
Thousands of camels were brought to Australia from Asia to transport people and goods.

## 1850s  OPENING UP THE WORLD
Thanks to George Stephenson's *Rocket*, passenger rail service expanded. A total of 800 kilometers (500 miles) of railroad existed in the United Kingdom in 1838. By 1860 this had increased to 16,000 kilometers (10,000 miles). Train services grew throughout Europe and Asia, too. By the 1890s, trains ran from Paris in France to Istanbul in Turkey.

## 1850s

In India camels pulled **stagecoaches** from town to town.

## 1869

The rickshaw was invented in Japan. Rickshaws were an early taxi service and are still popular in countries such as India.

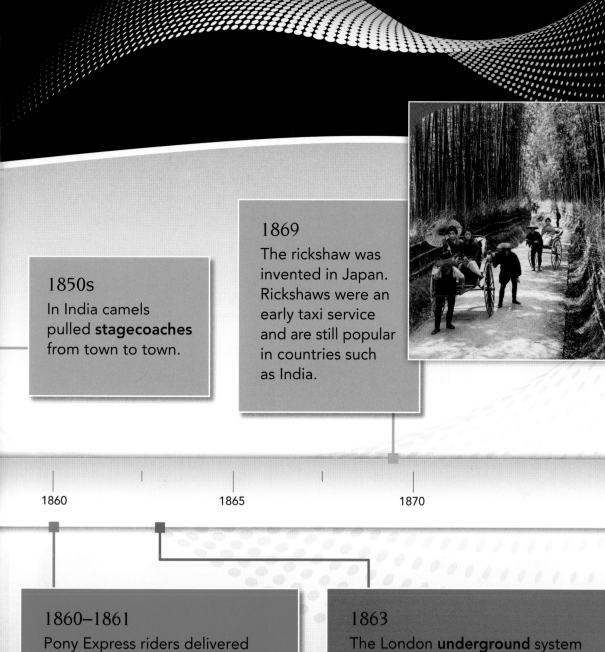

1860

1865

1870

## 1860–1861

Pony Express riders delivered the mail on horseback throughout the western United States. Riders could cover 400 kilometers (250 miles) a day.

## 1863

The London **underground** system carried 9,500,000 passengers during its first year. As cities grew, so did public transportation. Today, major cities such as New York, Rome (in Italy), and Mexico City (in Mexico) depend on buses, trains, and sometimes trams.

# Inventing the Car

The first cars were slow and expensive. In the 1880s, Karl Benz and Gottlieb Daimler invented gasoline **engines**. Other inventors raced to improve earlier designs. The age of the car had begun.

## 1885

In Germany, Gottlieb Daimler put his gasoline engine on a bicycle and made a motorcycle (left). He also built a car with four wheels using the same engine.

| 1870 | 1875 | 1880 | 1885 |

## 1870s

Three times a year, 15,000 camels traveled from Azerbaijan, on the Caspian Sea, to Turkey. Camel **caravans** carried as much as seven or eight ships could carry.

## 1885

Karl Benz of Germany invented a three-wheeled car with a gasoline engine.

**1890**

Bicycles became popular in Japan. Today, bicycles are used throughout the world.

**1898**

In the United States, the Stanley brothers' steam-powered car traveled at 56 kilometers (35 miles) per hour.

1890         1895         1900

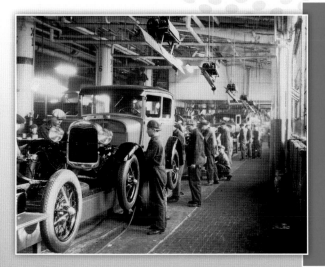

**1899   THE MODEL T**

The U.S. inventor Henry Ford started to make and sell cars. By 1913 they were being made on an **assembly line**, moving on a belt to workers who put the pieces together. Between 1908 and 1927, the Ford Motor Company produced half of all the cars made worldwide. By 1927 the company had made 15 million Model T cars.

# Flying

Once the Wright brothers invented a workable airplane, pilots eagerly took to the air.

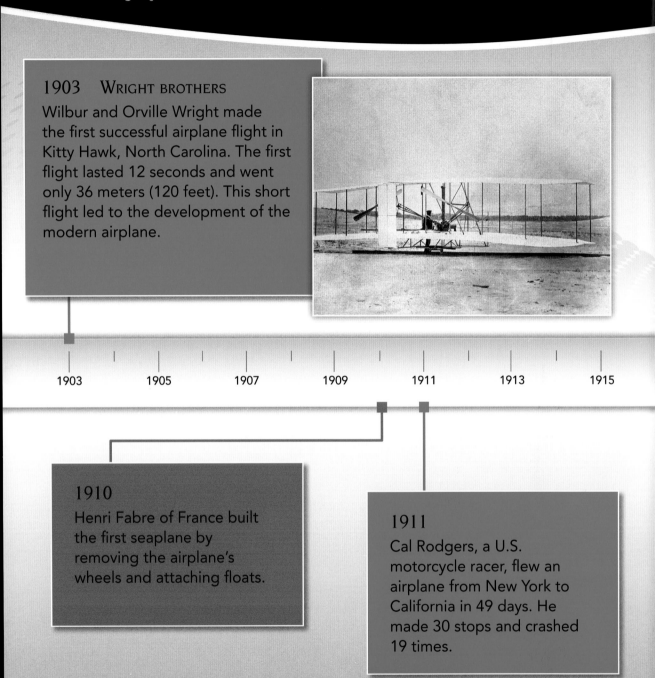

**1903   WRIGHT BROTHERS**

Wilbur and Orville Wright made the first successful airplane flight in Kitty Hawk, North Carolina. The first flight lasted 12 seconds and went only 36 meters (120 feet). This short flight led to the development of the modern airplane.

| 1903 | 1905 | 1907 | 1909 | 1911 | 1913 | 1915 |

**1910**

Henri Fabre of France built the first seaplane by removing the airplane's wheels and attaching floats.

**1911**

Cal Rodgers, a U.S. motorcycle racer, flew an airplane from New York to California in 49 days. He made 30 stops and crashed 19 times.

## 1918–1937

Balloon-like airships—also called zeppelins, blimps, and dirigibles—carried passengers across the Atlantic Ocean. In 1937 a German airship called the *Hindenburg* burst into flames over New Jersey. Thirty-six people were killed. This event brought airship passenger service to an end.

## 1920s

The first planes in West Africa were French mail carriers.

| 1917 | 1919 | 1921 | 1923 | 1925 | 1927 |

## 1927

The U.S. pilot Charles Lindbergh completed the first **solo** flight across the Atlantic Ocean. He flew from New York to Paris, France, in 33 hours and 29 minutes.

# Transporting Soldiers

During World War II (1939–1945), planes, ships, submarines, and trains became fighting machines. Inventors improved tanks, designed jets, and built aircraft carriers. Ships and trains transported soldiers to and from battlefields.

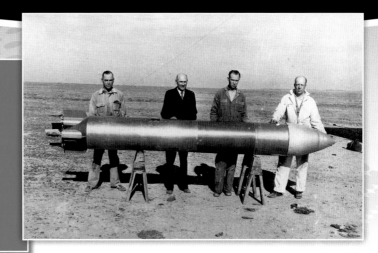

## 1930

Robert Goddard built a rocket test site in New Mexico. Rockets would later be used for spaceflight.

1930    1932    1934    1936    1938    1940    1942

## 1937   HELICOPTER

Igor Sikorsky, born in Russia in 1889, designed planes for the Russian Army. He moved to the United States in 1919 and designed a helicopter. By 1939 he had a working model that flew up and down as well as back and forth.

## 1939

A German test pilot flew the first jet-powered aircraft. The most successful German jet fighter could fly over 885 kilometers (550 miles) per hour.

## Late 1940s

Train tracks were repaired after World War II. Passenger services that had stopped during the war began again.

## Late 1950s

Passenger air travel increased.

1944    1946    1948    1950    1952    1954    1956

## 1939–1945

During World War II, the United States used 30 aircraft carriers. Planes landed and took off from the decks of the ships.

## 1956

In the United States, construction began on a system of highways across the country. These **interstate** highways now cover 75,440 kilometers (46,876 miles).

# Soaring into Space

In the 1950s, the United States and the **USSR** raced to see who could send a human being into space first. Today, countries in North America, Europe, and Asia work together to explore space.

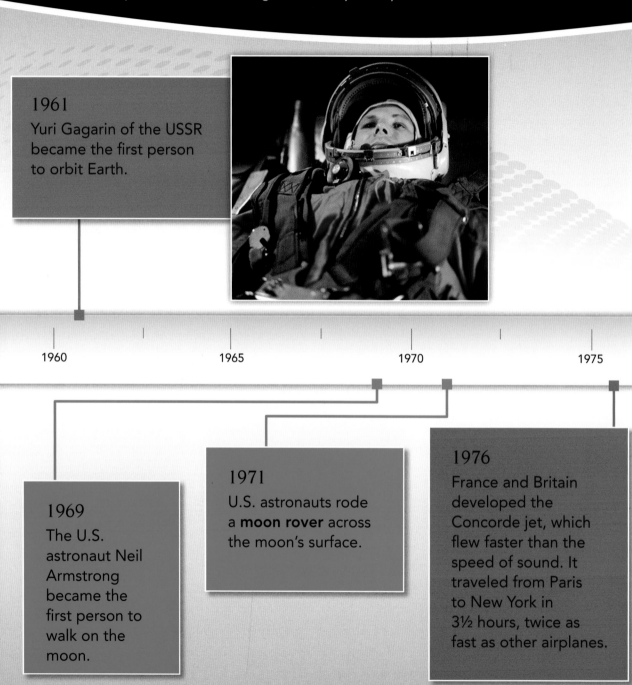

**1961**
Yuri Gagarin of the USSR became the first person to orbit Earth.

1960 | 1965 | 1970 | 1975

**1969**
The U.S. astronaut Neil Armstrong became the first person to walk on the moon.

**1971**
U.S. astronauts rode a **moon rover** across the moon's surface.

**1976**
France and Britain developed the Concorde jet, which flew faster than the speed of sound. It traveled from Paris to New York in 3½ hours, twice as fast as other airplanes.

## 1981 THE SPACE SHUTTLE

The United States launched the first space shuttle. It could land on a runway like an airplane and fly again. Shuttles carry people and supplies to the International Space Station. By 2015 shuttles will be replaced by newer spaceships.

## 1986

The space shuttle *Challenger* exploded on takeoff, killing everyone on board.

| 1980 | 1985 | 1990 |
|---|---|---|

## 1970s–present

People throughout Africa often rely on buses for transportation. Buses can be overcrowded.

# Going Green

Walking, cycling, or sailing rather than flying keeps the air clean. In the future, **vehicles** may get **energy** from the sun, wind, and magnets, rather than burning coal, gasoline, or oil.

## 2007
Bike-makers produced twice as many bicycles as cars. China leads the world in bicycle use.

## Present
Hybrid cars use electricity so they don't emit too many pollutants and gas so they can go at the speed and distance needed.

2000    2002    2004    2006    2008

## 2010
The giant wings of Switzerland's Solar Impulse use the sun's energy to power the plane.

## Present    MAGLEV TRAINS

Maglev (magnetic levitation) trains that operate in Japan and China are the world's fastest trains. They are called "green" trains because they use magnets for energy. Powerful magnets beneath the rail lift the train and pull it forward. By 2025 Japan plans to have a maglev train running between Tokyo and central Japan at over 500 kilometers (310 miles) per hour.

2010                    Future

## Present
Companies are planning the spaceships, space hotels, and space stations that tourists will need for space travel.

## Future
A moving science lab named *Curiosity* will explore Mars (above). Scientists from all over the world work to invent new ways to travel in outer space.

# Key Dates

**c. 98,000** BCE
Early people walk and drag items by hand.

**c. 6,000** BCE
Dugout canoes carry people along China's longest river, the Yangtze.

**c. 5,000** BCE
In North Africa, people use camels and donkeys to carry loads.

**c. 3,500** BCE
Sumerians invent the wheel.

**c. 700** CE
Vikings make fast wooden boats.

**c. 800** CE
Chinese traders start to use boats called junks to carry **cargo** to the market.

**c. 900–1000** CE
Horses travel farther and carry heavier loads once iron horseshoes and harnesses are invented.

**1492**
Christopher Columbus sails to America in a **carrack**.

**1500s–1800s**
Slave ships make over 39,000 trips from Africa to America.

**Late 1600s–1800**
Horses pull large, flat-bottomed boats called barges along the banks of **canals**.

**1700s**

Miners travel by canoe to the gold mines in Minas Gerais, the state that is the source of some of the biggest rivers in Brazil.

**1825**

George Stephenson builds a **locomotive** called the *Rocket*.

**1839**

Scottish **blacksmith** Kirkpatrick Macmillan invents the bicycle.

**1885**

German Karl Benz invents a three-wheeled car with a gasoline **engine**.

**1899**

Henry Ford founds his car company and sets up the **assembly line**.

**1903**

The Wright brothers make the first successful airplane flight.

**1961**

Russian cosmonaut Yuri Gagarin takes the first spaceflight.

**1969**

U.S. astronaut Neil Armstrong walks on the moon.

**1981**

The first space shuttle is launched from Florida.

**Present**

Maglev (magnetic levitation) trains that operate in Japan and China are the world's fastest trains.

# Glossary

**assembly line** moving belt in a factory that takes products being built to workers, who can then add the next part

**blacksmith** person who makes and repairs iron objects

**canal** long water channel built for traveling across large areas of land

**caravan** group of travelers journeying together for safety

**caravel** small Spanish or Portuguese ship with two or three masts

**cargo** trade goods carried on ships or other vehicles

**carrack** sturdy merchant ship used in the 1500s

**chariot** light, two-wheeled vehicle for one person, usually drawn by horses

**civilization** particular society or culture at a particular period of time

**dynasty** period of rule of a particular family

**energy** ability to do work

**engine** machine that burns fuel to turn energy into movement

**immigrant** person who comes to live permanently in a foreign country

**interstate** between different states in the United States. Interstate highways go from one state to another.

**locomotive** train engine that pulls carriages and other cars along

**Middle East** region that includes southwest Asia and northeast Africa

**moon rover** four-wheeled vehicle used by astronauts on the moon

**reed** straight stalk of grass

**solo** alone

**spoke** thin piece of a wheel that connects the center to the rim

**stagecoach** wagon pulled by an animal, taking passengers on a set route

**underground** railroad network that runs beneath the surface of Earth

**USSR** Union of Soviet Socialist Republics. The USSR later broke up into the Russian Federation and other countries.

**vehicle** means of transportation often having wheels or runners

**wheelbarrow** single-wheeled vehicle with handles, for moving heavy loads

# Find Out More

## Books

Curlee, Lynn. *Trains*. New York: Atheneum, 2009.

Furgang, Kathy. *Your Carbon Footprint: On the Move: Green Transportation*. New York: Rosen, 2009.

Graham, Ian. *Inventions in Transportation*. North Mankato, Minn.: QED, 2009.

Raum, Elizabeth. *Inventions That Changed the World: The History of the Car*. Chicago: Heinemann Library, 2008.

Zimmermann, Karl R. *Ocean Liners: Crossing and Cruising the Seven Seas*. Honesdale, Pa.: Boyds Mill, 2008.

## Websites

Learn more about space travel at this website.
**www.nasa.gov/audience/forkids/kidsclub/flash/index.html**

This website offers more information about the history of transportation.
**www.transitpeople.org/lesson/trancovr.htm**

Explore the parts of an airplane at this webiste.
**http://scifiles.larc.nasa.gov/kids/Problem_Board/problems/flight/parts2.html**

Learn more about the Wright Brothers and their invention of the airplane at this website.
**www.nasm.si.edu/wrightbrothers/**

## Places to visit

**Smithsonian National Air and Space Museum**
Independence Avenue Southwest & 6th Street SW
Washington, D.C. 20472
Tel: (202) 633-2214

**The Henry Ford Museum**
20900 Oakwood Boulevard
Dearborn, Michigan 48124
Tel: (313) 982-6001

# Index